Trees

Written by Jo Windsor

In this book you will see trees.

Look at the trees!

The trees are in the forest.

There are lots and lots of trees in this forest.

This forest is...
wet   Yes? No?
dry   Yes? No?

Trees in this forest grow and grow and grow!

There is lots of rain to help them grow.

There is lots of sun to help them grow.

Some trees grow where it is wet.

The trees are in the water.
It is very, very wet.

If there is no water, the trees will...

fall over   Yes? No?

grow   Yes? No?

not grow   Yes? No?

Look at the trees!

They are in the water, too.
Look at their roots.

The roots are not in the ground.
The roots are up out of the ground!

The roots are up out of the ground...

to get the sun   Yes? No?

to get out
of the water   Yes? No?

Here are lots of trees in the water. The roots grow up out of the water.

The roots help the trees stay in the water.

The water...

holds the trees   (Yes?) No?

makes the roots clean   Yes? (No?)

Look at the trees!
They are in a very hot place.

Trees in hot places can grow very tall.

They grow tall so animals cannot eat all the leaves.

Look at these tree trunks!

They are very fat.
The trees keep water inside them.

Index

forest 3, 4, 6, 8, 10

leaves 19

rain 6

roots . . 3, 8, 10, 14, 16

sun 7, 8

trunk 3, 20

water 12, 14, 16, 20

Labels

Look at the tree.

Put labels on this picture.

roots

branches

eyes

leaves

hands

trunk

Word Bank

rain

roots

sunshine

trunk